DR BINAY SINGH'S GUIDE TO

# LEADERSHIP TRAINING

# DR BINAY SINGH'S GUIDE TO LEADERSHIP TRAINING

DR BINAY SINGH

TWAGAA
HTTPS://TWAGAA.COM

TWAGAA
HTTPS://TWAGAA.COM

Mumbai (MH), India
Website: https://twagaa.com
Email: hello@twagaa.com

First published by TWAGAA INTERNATIONAL 2020


Title: Dr Binay Singh's Guide to Leadership Training

ISBN: 978-93-90488-29-2

First Edition
Published in India



Ordering Information:
Quantity sales: Special discounts are available on quantity purchases by corporations, associations, and others. For details, contact the publisher at the address or email above.

# ACKNOWLEDGEMENTS

I am very grateful to all the people in this beautiful world whose sincere and kind blessings have inspired me to write a book that I have dreamed about forever. In my lifetime, I have read many books on leadership written by renowned authors. I am thankful to all of them for being my mentors with their awesome teachings.

Here, in my book, I want to share my decades of experience in such a way that my dear readers will not only be inspired to be true leaders but also go forward and possess their assignments on this beautiful planet. There is no rarer commodity on this earth other than leadership.

My sincere gratitude to my parents who imbibed me with the best traits to live my life only for other people. I love to say with pride that "your happiness is my happiness." I have written this book to see all leaders succeed with happiness; no matter if they are economic leaders, political leaders or just leaders in their own personal lives.

Many thanks to all my friends across the globe. Special

thanks to my dear friend, Nick, who has been helping me for almost a year with his awesome guidance.

I am grateful to my family for giving me the opportunity and inspiration to work relentlessly for humanity.

I would also like to convey gratitude to my exclusive publisher Mr Amit Suri for his continued kind support.

# AUTHOR'S NOTE

*A true leader's success*
*lies in the growth of others.*
*- Dr Binay Singh*

To all the world leaders out there, let's create a world full of empathy, love and enthusiasm. No country can ever flourish if it stifles the potential of its men, women and future generations.

Great leaders always work with the tools they are given. We must use empathy, love and enthusiasm as tools to construct our lives. I am sure if we all become emotionally functioning adults, we can change the world for the better.

# CONTENTS

# INTRODUCTION

# WHAT YOU CAN ACHIEVE BY READING THIS GUIDE

They say that great leaders are not made, they are born. I tend to disagree with that statement because of my nearly two decades in the business world. Leaders come in all shapes, sizes and circumstances. There are definitely people in our world who are born with great leadership abilities, but that does not certify them to guide teams, business units or entire companies successfully. A leader has to combine their natural raw strengths with acquired skills from training, one-to-one mentorship and real-life experiences in order to know how to effectively lead. Becoming a leader requires considerable effort on the part of an individual. The basis of leadership training is not just assessing candidates to enter into a company's program to create the executives of tomorrow, but also understanding that each candidate should be taught and nurtured in different ways. It is a living, breathing experience, not a simple series of online courses and tests. It is that sort of elaborate functionality that makes leadership training both exciting when it is going well and frustrating when it is not. The purpose of this guide is to get you on the right track to becoming a great leader or alternatively, helping in your process of developing several great leaders. Leadership training helps current leaders and managers find more innovative ways to both develop and manage their employees, develop innovative business opportunities, and take on broader issues of society, relationships and the changing face of the workplace. Malleable, flexible, intelligent leaders have never been more important in the world than they are right now. Take a deep dive with me as we focus more specifically on what such leadership looks like and how to get the best candidates up to speed to take over the reins when the time comes.

Keep in mind that leadership training is not just something to take on when you are first promoted to a position where you manage other people or when you are seeking to start someone on a path towards a career in management. Leadership training can be beneficial for anyone in any industry: whether he is already in a leadership role, is being groomed for one, or thinking about taking that career direction.

# CHAPTER 1

# THE TRAITS THAT MAKE A GREAT LEADER

Leaders appear in all shapes and sizes. Some are in business, some in the military, some are in communities, and some are in the government. Regardless of what the environment looks like, they share certain elements in common that allow them to elevate their game and grow beyond where they started. It also allows them to successfully motivate their followers to adapt to their situation, pinpoint their goals, and find the path forward for them while projecting the idea of leadership and how it can be used to inspire, remain positive, and push past the obstacles that will inevitably arise. These traits do not make every leader a successful leader or a great leader, but they can be considered as a powerful base from which a great leader is built.

## 1. BEING A ROLE MODEL

Everyone wants their children to have a great role model - someone they look up to, emulate their behavior, and strive to take on the world in a similar fashion. Should we stop admiring people just because we have turned 18? Of course not! Role models can be even more valuable at the workplace than they are at home because there are fewer reinforcements required. A child might pick a famous actor, a singer, or an athlete as a role model and attempt to emulate their success and listen to their teachings on life. But that child also gets positive reinforcement from its parents, grandparents, other family members, teachers and from the community. Once we become adults, we typically aren't around all those natural positive influences anymore, which can lead to a decay in our behavior. A role model at work can not only show people how to act professionally in all things, but how to adapt to changes, setbacks, previously uncharted water, and the sort of transitions that take place in the business world that individual employees seldom, if ever, have any control over. Professional leaders inspire like-minded behavior in others that can encompass everything from respectful conduct, to correct business attire, to how to communicate in any number of different settings, to work ethic. How important is it to have a boss who inspires you and respects you? According to Builtin[1], almost 80% of employees quit their job because they don't feel appreciated by their boss. I like to consider myself a role model for my employees, and that begins with the way I come to work each day.

On Monday morning, when the workday begins, I don't

1. *https://goremotely.net/blog/leadership-statistics/*

come into my office with a slouch and a sigh, throw my briefcase on the desk, and moan, "Great, another Monday." Instead, I behave completely opposite, to the point that both coworkers and clients have called me "Mr. Positive". When they come to my office, or I go to meet them for a cup of coffee or a meeting, I always have the biggest smile on my face. I am a people's person, so every time I go to work knowing I'll be talking to people, and more importantly, helping their lives for the better, it makes me feel good. I realize that not every part of a leader's job is going to make them feel good, but I am hopeful that if you are training to be a leader or already are one, that the positives of your job outweigh the negatives. If they don't, you may be focusing on the wrong parts of your job or need a refresher in what leadership looks like.

Regardless, I know that when I show my passion, joy and commitment to my employees, it inspires them to fill their days with the same sort of positivity. Being professional in all things is one of the best ideas for a work environment. Think about it: if you are professional when dealing with a good or great client, they are going to want to work with you again because you're confident, respectful and committed to a relationship where both of you succeed. The ideal employee carries all of those qualities, but many of them don't practice them because they don't have a professional role model to show them how it's done. If you are the leader at your job and you are always in a bad mood - talking about clients behind their backs, gossiping about your subordinates, or complaining about the work you have to do - how can you expect anything but more of the same behavior from your employees? Be their guiding light. They don't have to do everything as well as you do, but modelling positive behavior can show sizable improvements in all of your employees over time.

## 2. MAKING AN IMPACT

It is incredible how many times you find leaders who act more like facilitators than leaders. They develop plans, assign positions to everyone, and then simply step back and watch the action unfold. That might be well if you are a teacher administering an exam, but the best leaders are doing so by example; they are leading the way, not watching from behind.

Too many leaders get comfortable in their roles and want to maintain the status quo. This is not really leading, but more like treading the water. In today's fast-paced business world, you cannot afford to fall behind. Technology , customer desires, and the rapid changes taking place in just about every industry mean that if you're not keeping pace, you're going to have a very hard time. Making an impact means developing a strategy, implementing it, and delivering the results. In my role as the head of a large shipping firm that pairs seafarers with appropriate companies and ships, I have the chance to make an impact every single day in every single interaction that I have. What an honor!

When I am working with a company, they are giving me the opportunity to find them crew members that will become the banner-holders of their name, their identity, and their brand. This is a huge responsibility and I never, ever, take it lightly. When I talk to seafarers, I am becoming their guide in an industry that is very competitive and that can be very competitive, especially if you are seeking to work internationally. These individuals are trying to get jobs, to build a career, and maintain their roles as providers for their families. How can I do anything but the best in every single action that I take? The higher you move up in the hierarchy of your own company, your individual actions and decisions will have an impact on more and more peoples' lives. You should be excited about that proposition; but also, extremely careful that you think beyond yourself and what makes sense for you to think of the larger scope and how your actions can cause ripples through your company and your industry.

## 3. FOCUSING ON A VISION

Tying in with the aforementioned point is the fact that if you don't have a destination in mind and a specific route to get there, you're going to wander aimlessly for a long time. Vision doesn't just refer to the place you want your business to reach, but the methodology you're going to use to ensure that you get there, along with the path you are going to take without any sort of deviations. This is where the qualities of leadership begin to include not just leading but doing what is right and morally sound. A company's goal might be to make as much money as possible every year, but how are they going to do it? One strategy might be to raise prices of those items which customers think as essential, or invent a membership fee that people have to use to purchase certain quantities of goods. But is that in line with the company's desire to be an ethical company which believes in its customers and wants them to succeed? It really comes down to knowing what a company stands for and how to instill that into everything that you do as a leader. If you can't honor the building blocks of the company, it is difficult to be a real leader.

Focusing on building your culture is imperative to be a good leader who inspires others to work for the company. According to Forbes[2], about 70% of employees in the United States are unhappy with their job due to what they see as a failing job of poor management. When I am hiring for new positions, it's great to get to know potential employees and ask them about their background, their experience, and all that. But I also want to know about their beliefs - how they work with other people, and if they see a position as just a job to earn a paycheck or as a venue in which they can do something special. For instance, as listed on my company's website, we itemized several visions that we have on how we will address our clients, when we will be available to them, and what our goals are for the long-term. A good leader not only shares these goals with his or her followers but also has them specifically for the company. That vision can be whatever you want to make it - from growing your staff from three people to thirty people; or making your department a bastion of diversity and free thought; or to

2. *https://goremotely.net/blog/leadership-statistics/*

simply have everyone follow the Golden Rule and work every day to treat each other with respect, kindness, and love. A good leader should not only have a vision, but also live it and commend others for doing so.

## 4. ENCOURAGE COLLABORATION

For the first six years of his NBA career, Michael Jordan was undoubtedly the best basketball player on the entire planet. So why didn't his team, the Chicago Bulls, win any NBA titles in that time frame? Because Jordan was the best player in a sport where only one player is never enough to do everything and win. No matter how strong a leader you are, you're not going to be able to solve every problem by yourself, nor should you want to. No matter how unique an idea you have of yourself, a smart leader is someone who recognizes that the team around him is also full of quality individuals who are capable of having creative, powerful ideas that can solve problems and figure out solutions to what customers want. What's better, having one mind devoted to great ideas or several? That part of leadership is one of the most overlooked.

Too many leaders believe that they, and they alone, should be steering the ship, with everyone else just doing the dirty work and the manual labor. That's nothing but taking away from what the spirit of leadership is. It's not merely having everyone follow your lead, but rather pointing them in the right direction and letting them blossom on their own to see what ideas, solutions, and masterstrokes they can form for the good of the team and the company.

Collaboration is not just a good feeling but a leading indicator of how well a company is functioning. According to SalesForce[3], 86% of employees and executives list a failure to collaborate or ineffective communication as the top reason for failures in the workplace. At my office, I have the most experience in the industry out of anyone working there, but does that mean that only Dr Singh can come up with viable strategies when problems arise? Certainly not! I encourage my staff to speak their minds whenever they have something to share which can contribute towards making us a better company. When you're a leader, yours does not need to be the loudest voice or the voice that is heard the most; indeed, you could consider that more often than not,

---

3. *https://blog.learningwithbiz.com/9-amazing-statistics-power-of-teamwork#:~:text=According to a survey by,depend on technology to collaborate.&text=Workplace collaboration can increase successful innovation by 15%.*

a great leader needs to stay quiet in order to hear everyone else's voices, take their opinions, weigh them against your own knowledge, and then make the best decision. There's a big difference between being a leader and becoming a dictator.

## 5. BEING POSITIVE

No one is saying you have to be a cheerleader and tell everyone how amazing they are all day long, but if the person in charge does not appear to want to be at work and is not enjoying it, then how in the world can you expect anyone else to feel any different? Clearly going to work is an experience that many of us wish was voluntary instead of mandatory. There is also an old saying, '*if you find something that you love and can find a way to get paid for it, you'll never work a day in your life.*' If you've advanced to the management level of your industry, then I sincerely hope that you feel passionate about it and aspire to do great things. So many leaders fail their employees by getting too tied down in the mechanism of becoming the one in charge, as it often involves a lot more responsibility and a lot more bureaucracy. But neither of those things should be doled out on your employees, nor any negative emotions you might have as a result of doing all that extra work. Both positivity and negativity emotions are contagious at the workplace.

Take two minutes and think about who was the best boss you've ever had.

*Did you get his/her picture in your mind?*
*What did they do best?*
*How did they lead?*
*Did the work seem more fun than other jobs?*

That's the secret! A positive boss makes you want to work hard because they know how to motivate you, whether it be in from incentives, the camaraderie, or some other factor. A negative boss can make normal days feel like marathons and drain the life out of even the best employees.

A positive boss excels at finding the best in every situation while a negative boss doesn't even bother trying at all. As I said earlier, a lot of people call me "Mr. Positive" for the way that I approach the day. But what happens when external forces make it tough to be so positive? I think back on the events of March 2020 when the coronavirus went from something affecting only China to a pandemic taking root in every country of the world - forcing people to stay at home for weeks and months, and disrupting every facet of our society. As of 10th January 2021, more than 1.15 million cases had been confirmed in Ukraine and almost 20,000 people had lost their lives. From March to June 2020, foreigners were banned from entering Ukraine. There have been close to 90 million cases worldwide and 1.93 million deaths. In my beloved homeland of India, more than 10.5 million have contracted the virus, and more than 151,000 of them have died from it.

*How did I keep my staff positive during these times?*
*How did I tell the seafarers, who trusted us to ensure them great work, that things would continue to be okay in the face of so much uncertainty?*

For starters, I did not change my daily routine of exercise and meditation. Those things make me start off the day right, no matter what I am facing or where I must go. Second, I tamped down on rumor-mongering, and being fearful of things I did not know or could not predict. Third, I told my staff, my clients, and my contacts that the world was going to keep turning no matter what happened with COVID-19. People weren't going to stop needing the things that are shipped; in fact, they would probably need them even more now since everyone was suddenly staying at home. We are in an industry where we serve others, and in a time of crisis, that role is magnified.

Being positive does not mean making false promises or throwing a blanket of "*everything will be fine*" over everyone. It involves being transparent, taking on new situations and problems one at a time, and being dedicated to your commitment of taking care of your employers and those who look to you for guidance. Together, we took on each new day of the COVID-19 pandemic as a team, gathered all the facts, and then made decisions that honored our own vision, our company's initiatives, the safety procedures that were implemented internationally, nationally and inside our industry, and went to work with the same passion and compassion we were putting forward every other day. In this unprecedented event, I was not just the captain of the ship, but also the sailor manning the rudder, ensuring that we kept a straight course through uncharted waters.

# CHAPTER 2

# LEARNING FROM EXPERIENCE

The term *trial by fire* is a pretty serious thing when you think about it. It originated in the Middle Ages when people had to go through a rite of passage that often involved walking barefoot over hot coals. It seems like a terrible, painful ordeal to most of us, although the secret back then - and even today - is that our feet have a tough outer layer of skin that can protect us against hot temperatures if we move fast enough across them. The experience of walking across hot coals is one that you will never forget for the rest of your life and it will teach you multiple lessons, including how to overcome fear, how to take risks, and that there is a method to its madness; if you move quickly and don't freeze up, you will not actually get burned.

Of course, there is no way to understand that little secret until you've actually walked across the coals. You hear about the same kind of thing when you read about the history of military commanders - no matter how much training they have, no matter how many years of training at an academy they have gone through, until they are in their first real battle with bullets flying and people dying, they don't really understand what war is all about. While a business might not be as intense as an all-out military conflict, the lesson remains the same - until you've lived it, you can't understand it. A formal education is very important to becoming a leader.

I know that there is no way I could have ever succeeded in the shipping industry without having attended the Maritime Academy in Ukraine. But that is just one piece of the puzzle. The theories and exercises that you take on in building your education are not only eye-opening but form the base of your knowledge when going into a leadership role. But once you are there, you will find more times than not that no leadership issue, or really any issue related to your business, can fit into a nice little package that you can easily solve using a textbook. The difference of course is that the real world is full of people and events that do not fall into neat little categories. Do you think there is any textbook in the world that has a unit on what to do as a business leader in the event of a global pandemic that shuts down huge swathes of the global economy? Of course not! Thus, it fell on individual leaders to decide how to best chart the course through these bizarre times and into recovery. If you were new to leadership around March 2020, you might have felt overwhelmed by the circumstances. However, it is not just your experiences as a leader you must draw from, but your experiences in total. Things that have stuck with you from your earliest days have stuck with you for a reason - they introduced you to something, made you feel a certain way or gave you a new experience that your brain determined to be valuable enough to create a long-lasting memory of. That sort of impact should not be taken lightly. It is part of playing your hunches and going with your gut that so many leaders are successfully following. Leadership experience is not only created on the factory floor or in the boardroom, but in the classroom, in your own home, on the street, and at any previous position you've held either as an employee, a volunteer or simply as the member of a group. What do I mean by this? Let me go through a few examples from my own life to give you a better grasp of it.

When I was first attending a university here in Odessa, I looked like a model student on the outside. I was first in my class in learning to speak Russian, I was helpful to other students, I was respectful of my teachers and I was studying hard to honor the sacrifices my parents had made to get me to this remarkable university, to learn a new trade and begin a new life. But after a few months, a change came over me. I started dating a young woman who was not interested in getting a good education, contributing to society, or helping others. She wanted to have fun, get drunk and play around. She was very beautiful, and I was young and very impressionable. When she took an interest in me, pleasing her and spending time with her became the most important part of my life; everything else not only took a backseat but was not even in the same vehicle as she and I. When I was not with her, I was counting down the hours until I saw her again. When we were together, I was wasting my money buying her drinks and gifts, wasting my time taking her out when I should have been studying or attending classes, and wasting my brain cells consuming way too much alcohol. It almost cost me everything. I couldn't get through one of my exams, required to advance to the next level of school. Finally, with the help of friends and people who invested in my success, I was able to shake free of that bad influence and to get my life back on the right track. In the short term, I was horrified by the way I was acting and wished I could have gone back and broken up with her the first day we met, or just not met her at all. In the long-term, my hindsight is much different. I am thankful for that experience, as painful as it was. It showed me how easily it can be to get sidetracked by something that makes you feel good in the short term but is really keeping you away from being the person you should be in the long term. That helped me tremendously in both my personal and professional life. I am grateful to the Almighty that I went through this painful and embarrassing time because of which I am able to see similar warning signs in other people; whether they are employees, friends, or clients. In these instances, I am not only capable of seeing the signs of stress, but also intervene to help them. People who have never been in that situation might not do the same thing for the fear of upsetting someone or overstepping their boundaries.

A second situation where experience guided me to be the type of leader I am today, stems from my first job in the industry and a story I have told many times over. That first job was for an industry startup in Ukraine that was trying to dig into its own niche in the recruiting industry. It believed that niche was to secure clients from India and get them under contract, thus gaining lots of influence on the Indian shipping industry in the Black Sea region. Since I am an Indian and fluent in the Hindi language, they first hired me to do the recruiting work but then began to expand my sphere of influence to include meet-and-greets with prominent Indian shipping representatives when they come to visit Ukraine or even on trips back to India. What a thrill for a young man! Normally a person of my age and lack of experience would likely have been relegated to some back office, crunching numbers and analyzing data out of the public eye. I was, after all, still a student when I first started working at this company. My diligence and effort were being rewarded with a small salary and help with my school fees, and the proper paperwork I needed in place to remain eligible for work in Ukraine. Imagine being in my shoes; having the leadership of the company tell you that they wanted you to meet the owners and business leaders of several big companies in the industry who are from your homeland! On top of that, you had been told that you would be coming along on business trips to your homeland with all expenses paid for! Moreover, that would become a vital cog in the future of the company, with a rapid ascent through the ranks and further monetary compensations. When you've been around the block a few times, you understand that this is flattery and falls under the category of 'if something seems too good to be true, it probably is.' But I was young and naive and full of myself, so I believed every single thing they told me, and just assumed that I was so marvellously intelligent and talented that they wanted me to work there, forever.

Of course, while reading this book you can probably discern at least some of the truth of the situation. They were not interested in me for any reason other than fairly cheap labor and a token Indian employee to parade in front of the business leaders they hoped to impress. Indeed, they would make sure I was in the office anytime an executive came to visit, and one of my bosses even took me on a business trip to several Indian cities to ensure I was seen and those companies knew how pro-Indian the startup was. Then, as they say, the other shoe dropped. When I asked for paid leaves to attend my father's funeral, I was denied and told that if I went, I would be fired. Additionally, when they had secured all the contracts they could from India, I was allowed to go and the owners made their best efforts to have me deported so I could not work for another company in Ukraine. Those were some of the darkest days of my life, but they also were some of the most important experiences to draw from when I became a leader. Such an experience left me vowing that I would never ever treat any employee with the sort of disdain and disrespect that I had experienced. It made me value people to the point that I put them forth in everything I do - whether someone who has started working for me yesterday or a client with whom I have been with for twenty years. That experience from my early 20s still mandates the way I do things into my 40s because it has altered my entire perspective on how a business should be run and how people should be treated. Make sure you do the same when you are moving into a leadership role or training someone else to do so. The experiences that form our moral code are very important and should be incorporated into our style of leadership.

## CHAPTER 3

# ADVANTAGES OF BEING A TRUE LEADER

If history has taught us anything, it's that not everyone is cut out to be a leader. Some people become leaders by fate or circumstance, though they are not qualified, and it shows in their behavior. Others become leaders for the wrong reasons - the pursuit of power, money or control over others. This can be just as bad, or worse, than those who wind up in the position without qualifications or the desire to do so. So what is the point of being a leader when it seems like so many stumble and fall when they attempt to do so? For me, there are five wonderful rewards for being a leader that I experience at least on a weekly basis, if not more often.

1. ***Being admired and having your opinion valued.*** If you desire a leadership role, you likely have lots of ideas and inspirations that you would like to try out, test, implement, and refine. If you're the boss, you can do this on your own accord, but you'd prefer to have your thoughts and ideas be something that motivates other people, and have them interested in what you have to say and what you are capable of. When you start to command your own confidence - how you present yourself, how you inspire others - people will gravitate towards you and value what you are saying, because you

are the one saying it. Look at someone like the late, great Steve Jobs, former CEO of Apple. He dealt in innovation, and the way that he presented the company's products at its signature showcase events made people seek out his presence and want to be part of his projects because of the sense of power and vision that he gave off. Because of the presence he began to command, Jobs could really innovate and push the envelope on a host of different ideas - even the ones that might not have been given the green light in other circumstances. I think that if you are a visionary in your field, you owe it to yourself and your ideas to work in a leadership position so that you can have the following and the landscape to accomplish those ideas. Don't sell yourself or your ideas short. The best way to vocalize them and breathe them into life is by putting yourself in the position to put the spotlight on them.

**2. *Building your confidence to take on bigger things.***

Have you ever read the biography or an autobiography of a world leader? They are fascinating to read because you can see the entire history from their earliest aspirations to their place on the world stage. What you will often see is that it is not a situation where someone went from having a small-time position to suddenly leading a huge amount of people or being given a massive amount of responsibility, but where a person's success in the first step gets them promoted to a bigger role. Each new challenge is not viewed as a burden but an opportunity, and they pull on their experience from the previous positions to make the next one even better. These incremental gains and successes build up a leader's confidence. And regardless of how big the task is or how high the stakes are, they can succeed because they have done this before. Every great leader at some point was giving their first speech, engaging in their first debate, or presenting their first business plan. Taking those successes and building on them eventually gives a leader the confidence to do anything.

3. ***Bringing out the best in others.***

Very few people are talented in everything. Those who are, become legends. For the rest of us, we might have one thing we're really amazing at - writing, graphic design, math, science, innovation, people skills, etc. One of the best advantages of being a great leader is the ability to draw those talents out from other people and help them harness the good of everyone. If you are a leader, you are likely to know the best skills that each of your staff members have. One might be a brilliant artist, another a whiz at supply chain, and the third who is a master of communication. The best plan a leader can have is to put each of these people in roles that suit them best and allow them to make the greatest impact on their work in particular and the work itself in general. In my company, I don't ask our IT specialist to start answering the phones and talking to our clients, because I know that is not where his expertise lies. The more one leads, the more one can see where their followers' strengths and weaknesses lie. Once you can start identifying these characteristics, you take on the role of something akin to the coach or manager of a championship-winning athletic team, or to be even more abstract, a person with an eye for puzzles who is sitting in front of a box with 5,000 pieces and starts going to work immediately. You can have a new project in front of you and immediately identify which members of your team should take on each specific part of it. This also begins to showcase itself in the ability to see which members of your team work best together, which allows you to pair them up in smaller groups to take on more intensive projects that require more independent thought and critical thinking.

When you can start doing this sort of delegation of responsibilities, you free yourself up to do the things that a leader does best - focus on the overall vision, look ahead to the future, and take the steps necessary to accelerate your team's journey to reach it. One of my favorite quotes about this type of leadership comes from former American First Lady Elanor Roosevelt, who once said, "*A good leader inspires people to have confidence in the leader. A great leader inspires people to have confidence in themselves.*"

4. ***Leaders can help people grow beyond what they believe their own limitations are.***

If you've ever had a teacher tell you that they see a lot of potential in you, then you have been touched by a leader. Our teachers are the first leaders most of us encounter outside of our homes. They are the people who have a certain set of training, a lot of experience, and the ability to teach those skills to us if we are willing to learn. A lot of times, teachers see us as a raw lump of clay waiting to be shaped into something better. We might doubt our own ability to do the things they think we can, but it's only because we don't have the same vision, at least not yet. A teacher will often see that we have talent in a particular subject or for something like debate, dance, art, music, math or coding, and reach out to us to find ways to augment it and help us refine that talent. When the proper adjustments are made, we end up shining brighter than we would have thought possible. Leaders are the same way, particularly as they grow more confident and more experienced. As a leader matures, they are able to see similarities in themselves and others. This makes them see the potential in others for becoming future leaders. The same thing might happen with someone who has great creative skills, great people skills, great supply chain skills, or great strategizing skills. When a leader recognizes these skills, it is not just a good idea, but their responsibility for the betterment of their team as well as the entire organization to find ways to motivate the team members towards better things. Even if it means ultimately losing that team member to another department or even another company, it is still the right thing to do as it is their responsibility to get the most out of everyone.

**5. *Great leaders go for it.***

I beg your pardon if it sounds like I am beating my own chest here, but my life is richer, fuller and more satisfying because I made the decision two decades ago to become a leader. It was right after I had been fired by the company that had sold me up the river in order to get as many contracts from Indian companies as possible. I was low on funds, I was not sure I was going to be allowed to stay in the country and I was also full of doubt. It would have been very easy for me to just accept this defeat and start over at another company, probably near or at the lowest rung of the ladder. That would have been OK. I would have been able to make enough money to keep my apartment and slowly built my way back up. But I didn't want to do that. I didn't want to run the risk of having the same thing happen twice. I didn't want to have to live off someone else's whims if I was a good enough person, or to not get promoted. So, I decided to take the bolder route and went for it. I decided to start my own company and become the type of leader that I wanted to work for, the kind of leader who was going to value people and their contributions way more than the almighty dollar, the bottom line or the thrill of competition. That meant starting from scratch, with very little in the bank and very little to rely on outside of my own wits and my network of contacts in the shipping industry. With luck, prayer and many wonderful friends, I was able to turn that idea into a business that is now about to enter its third decade of service. I love that I made that choice. I love the zest for life I am able to inject into my day-to-day work and the ability to make other peoples' lives happier. I do not know if I would have ever gotten to this point if I had not taken the plunge and decided to become a leader. It might have been that I would have moved higher and higher in a company, but would I have ever reached this zenith? Would I ever have been able to separate myself and start my own company where my morals and visions were the main focus? I don't know what the answer is to that question, because I could not risk it. I knew when it was time to take the reins myself and to take over the leadership role.

# CHAPTER 4

# CHALLENGES OF BEING A TRUE LEADER

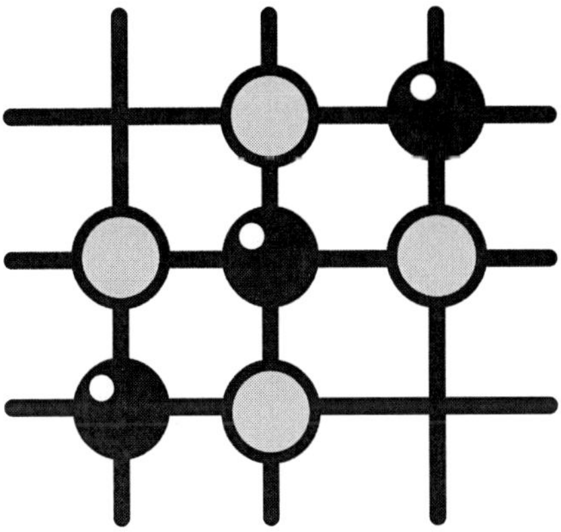

With the thrill and excitement of being a real leader, comes the difficulties that seek to mire your success and slow down your ability to deliver on your promises. Neither the world nor the workplaces are perfect environments, and there are many impediments that can trip up anyone's drive and determination. Often, how challenges are handled is far more of a testimony to a great leader then measurables of success. Success can often come without a strong leader, although sustainable success is more difficult to achieve without a top dog who knows his or her stuff. When something breaks, someone quits, there's a change at the top, a natural disaster disrupts the workflow or, say, a once-in-a-lifetime pandemic takes shape: that's when the truly great leaders step to the forefront, roll up their sleeves, and get to work.

These eight challenges are among the most difficult ones for any leader, and the way how a person responds to them separates the bad from the good, and the average from the elite.

***1. Dealing with Difficult People***

I might be Mr. Positive, but even I know that not everyone else is going to be in a good mood when I deal with them. I have experienced it with clients, with business partners, with officials, and yes, even with members of my own staff. Some don't realize that they are being difficult, and that makes them a lot easier to handle - you can adjust your personality, the way you speak, the way you go through your workflow to avoid the parts of the interaction that makes them difficult. For instance, if a customer never returns your phone calls, make a point to stop by their office to tie down contracts and secure payment from them. If they have a problem paying their invoice on time, incentivize their being on time with a slight discount on your next deal together. Be smart and figure out how to turn their weakness into a strength. If a person you work with is difficult but doesn't realize it, expand or contract their responsibilities as much as you can so the thing that upsets or angers them is something they do not have to do at all or not very frequently. Of course, there are also difficult people who are being difficult on purpose, either to try and work a better deal, because they are trying to gain an upper hand over you, or simply because they like making other people squirm. There is only one real solution for interacting with these kinds of people, regardless of whether they are clients, coworkers or customers, and that is to kill them with kindness. No matter how they approach you, your only reaction should be with respect, politeness, and a smile. Do not let them get under your skin or push your buttons; no matter how much they frustrate you with their antics, actions, words, or refusal to do what they promised.

***2. Pressure***

Work can seem like fun when everything is going smoothly and everyone is getting along, but that can go by the wayside quickly when pressure becomes a problem. Even though leaders are often the top dog at the company, just as often they are not. Which means, having to answer to a higher authority, a deadline, a budget, or the ebb and flow of the industry. The pressure of being the boss can be more debilitating, than anyone else's, if the weight of such a task falls solely on you. Your employees might have to deal with you, but your job is about getting results, which can be stressful when that means relying on many other people or external factors that you may or may not have control over. Time is usually the deadliest sort of pressure faced by any leader - how to do a great job by beating the clock?! Most leaders combat this difficulty by breaking projects and tasks up into smaller more manageable "chunks" that can be accomplished in order or in advance of a deadline. Pressure is when you come to see what your team is made of, and exactly how much you trust them to do a great job when you're not looking from over their shoulder or holding their hand. If you're a leader who cannot let go of the steering wheel and let someone else have a turn, it's always going to be a stressful situation. Pressure situations are the type when leaders really see what they are made of as well as what their teams are made of.

### *3. Letting Go of an Employee*

Most leaders cite this as being the very worst part of their line of work. Sometimes it's easier if the person wants to quit or has figured out another job they want to take, but unfortunately it often comes down to the leader - that's you - to terminate someone's contract. We'd all like to avoid such moments, but we would not be a good leader to the rest of our employees and team members if we devalued their work by letting someone who is just "getting by" or who is detrimental to our cause, to continue working for us. Leaders often follow their gut feelings, and when someone is not working, you usually know. That being said, when the time comes for a termination, you must have all your facts in hand,

and be as transparent as possible to prevent any sort of overspill of emotion or any movement on the part of the person being let go that would allow them to accuse you of having a grudge or a prejudice against them. Handle it with dignity, class and respect, and you can't go wrong.

**4. *The Bearer of Bad News***

As a leader, you're going to know the ins and outs of your business unit, the company itself and everything going on a bit earlier than everyone else. It means that you might have to deliver the news that others may not like and suffer through the negative reactions. There will be talk of layoffs, salary reductions, a loss of health benefits or Paid Time Off, news of employees leaving, news of clients deciding not to renew contracts, or things coming down from the board of directors that everyone should update their resumes which might make them worried about getting fired. The one thing I have found the most is employees value honesty more than anything else. Even if you have the worst news ever, such as your branch is closing, 50% of employees are being laid off, or the COVID-19 pandemic is forcing everyone to be furloughed for the next six months, your employees would much rather have the truth up front than be fed a series of half-truths from now until the moment the hammer actually does fall. Not telling the truth while delivering bad news damages your reputation and your brand as a leader. This is a very unlikely time you're going to serve a leader. Make sure that you are always being truthful and respectful when delivering news that won't be well-received.

### 5. *Staying Motivated*

Remember the first day of the new work year? How eager you were to get going? Maybe you bought coffee and donuts for the whole team, or you took everyone out to lunch, or brought them a new clock for their desks. It's so easy to be excited and motivated for the task at hand on that first day back from a vacation, or when you know you're about to close a big deal, or because you know your boss is preparing for performance reviews. A certain lack of lustre is more common when it's the middle of summer and you already took your leave, or you just missed on a big contract and now have to go back to the drawing board, or your prize employee who you were grooming to take over as manager one day just took another job with your chief competitor. Depression can sink in fast, malaise right alongside it in the flow of a business day.

How do you then stay on an even keel so that you can keep your employees and followers doing likewise? The biggest key is to treat every day as the same from a personal point of view. Prepare for your time in the office in the same fashion, starting with going to be on time the night before, getting exercise the next morning, doing things like using a gratitude journal or meditating before you head out to work. The work might not be as exciting some days as others, but it's all part of a bigger plan to succeed and make your clients, customers, employees and bosses happy with your work and satisfied with the results. I like to think about how going on a vacation is exciting even though some parts of it are quite dull. Let's say I am flying home to India from Ukraine. Well, I know right away that the time it takes me to actually get the airport and through security is not going to be fun and while I don't have to like it, I do have to stay motivated to ensure I have my ticket and passport, and that I follow all the safety procedures. The plane ride can be a nice time to read or listen to music, but it's just another long time with not much going on. Of course, when I land in India, it is still a long haul to get my luggage, grab a taxi and get to my mother's house to rejoice and celebrate with her. The end definitely justifies the means in this situation. It is worth all the slow moments and repetitive processes to get to the end result. So it is with dull moments in your team. Eventually, I will be where I want to be, just like eventually all the monotonous parts of your team's work will pay off with the success you were craving when you first took a project on.

### *6. Culture problems*

Culture is a must in a successful organization. You must be a leader in whatever culture your company has put together to guide its moral compass along the road to business success. These principles are not just buzzwords that the company's founders, its board of directors or even you, if you're a part of the committee that breathes life into such things, can develop. When the culture is put in place, it is for everyone to study, learn and abide by. There are not different sets of rules for different people in the organization. You might notice that particularly long-toothed employees often blanch at adopting new policies or new ways of doing things. You must be able to temper the balance between what has come before and what exists now, so that you are respectful of someone's long service without giving them a free pass to do whatever they want to. This can involve work processes, handling technology upgrades, collaborations; really anything at all that defines how the work is done and how the people are treated. When there is a problem with someone not willing to live up the culture they have signed for when they started to work at your firm, or someone who keeps slipping back into old habits, you have to practice a firm, methodical process to move them back onto the right track. It can start with simple communications, that update to requests, then a structured series of meetings and requirements to ensure it is met. Not everyone has to have the same opinion on everything, but they need to be able to maintain the standards that the company has built to do the business.

### *7. Being Liked and Respected*

One of my favorite American TV programs is "The Office". In this TV series, actor Steve Carrell pretends to follow the ups and downs of working in a paper company on the East Coast of the United States. Mr. Carrell plays the manager, Michael Scott, who is much more interested in having fun during the day than doing real work. In one episode, the cameraman asks him if he would rather be loved or feared as the boss and he replies, "Both. I want them to be scared of how much they love me." This is very good humor but also paints a picture of what some leaders struggle with. They want their employees to like them and be friendly with them, but also do what they say at any and all the times. Most of us do not have friends like that, do we? The fact of the matter is, plenty of your employees might not like you; but if they respect the kind of boss you are, you will stand the best chance of being successful as a leader and have them be successful members of your team. Respect means they understand why you make the decisions you do; they feel like you are serving the best interests of the company and the employees, and that you are going to give everyone a fair share of doing their best work. That's more than most people ever get at a job, and is exactly what most people want from their leader. Of course, many leaders get greedy and want everyone to invite them along for Happy Hour and to social events and get a Christmas card and all that good stuff. This is far less important than the respect factor, but some leaders lose their way in their pursuit of being liked, to the point of it affecting the way they lead. If one of your employees gives off the vibe of someone you would like to be friends outside the office, it can be very tempting to make work more fun for this individual, give them special privileges, or engage them in more activities than their position calls for. These are big no-nos for a quality leader, as when employees see you playing favorites, they will have a greatly reduced opinion of you. Remember, you're not trying to win any sort of popularity contest. You're trying to put together the best team - yourself included - to get the job done to its very highest level of accomplishment.

**8. *When Things Don't Work Out***

You and your team have spent the last six weeks crafting a killer proposal that you know is going to knock the client's socks off. Everyone works hard and everyone comes in the last two weekends before the presentation to make sure everything is as good as it can be. You sent it off the morning it's due and everyone is high-fiving and hugging over the successful thing you've created. A few days later you get the big phone call from the client everyone has been waiting for and hear that it's not what they wanted and they're going in another direction. It's a crushing blow, but it doesn't have to take the wind out of your team's sails and make you feel like a failure as a leader. Things don't always go your way, but it should not diminish how you feel as a leader or how your team feels overall. Not a single one of us can influence what happens outside of our own bodies, minds and souls. When others decide the work we have done is not up to the mark or they do not need it to be done anymore, it can be tough not to feel like a failure. But there is not a single company in the world that is successful every time it goes after a project. You have to temper your disappointment that the contract or project did not go your way with the idea of how well everyone worked together, how good the idea generation was, and how excited everyone was for the next project to roll down the tunnel. Tell yourself and your employees that practice makes us perfect.

# CONCLUSION

## LEADERSHIP IN THE 21ST CENTURY

By the time you read this, we will probably be nearing or beyond the one-year anniversary of the COVID-19 pandemic global shutdown; with countries all over the world still trying to find and adjust to whatever this new normal is. In the world that nobody could have expected, leadership is now more important than ever. Leaders must be flexible, willing to adapt to change on the fly, understand that things are not going to be the same as they used to be, and focus on making their employees, clients, partners and customers as comfortable as possible in order to satisfy their needs; ensuring that they have the right mindset to do the best work and get the finest results. The greatest organizations and communities of tomorrow are going to be the ones motivated and inspired by the best leaders. Will you be one of them?

# ABOUT THE AUTHOR

Dr Binay Kumar Singh, Founder & CEO of *Singh Marine Management Ltd.* in Odessa (Ukraine) and Founder & President of *Federation of Global Maritime Community,* is an entrepreneur, author, and public speaker. His life mission is to serve the world's communities and guide everyone through positivity, love, and enthusiasm. This is reflected in his simple and timeless life philosophy: "Treat people as you like to be treated."

Dr Singh has a Master of Science in Marine Navigation and a Doctorate of Philosophy. He is a globally recognized expert in international shipping with over two decades of experience. Dr Singh is also taking wonderful measures for the needy community of the society as well. His new project with the name "Selfless Fund" is specifically targeted to help those who are in need. Dr Singh has also launched his new company GSR which is going to bring innovations to the shipping and maritime industry. His efforts for the shipping industry as well as for the society is an example of his generosity and selflessness.

He enjoys pursuing multiple passions like singing, dancing, playing the piano and the accordion, and keeping healthy by practicing yoga and CrossFit.

Email: binay@drbinaysingh.com
Website: https://drbinaysingh.com

# MORE BOOKS BY DR BINAY SINGH

THE ART OF MARITIME MANNING
MY INSIGHTS
DR BINAY SINGH
THE ART OF NEGOTIATION
DR SINGH'S INSIGHTS
DR BINAY SINGH
THE ART OF SMARTPHONE-LIFE BALANCE
DR SINGH'S INSIGHTS
DR BINAY SINGH
ODESSA
MY CITY, MY HOME
DR BINAY SINGH
DIGITAL ADDICTION
KEEP YOURSELF AND YOUR FAMILY SAFE
DR BINAY SINGH
THE ART OF TEAM MANAGEMENT
DR BINAY SINGH
THE ART OF LEADERSHIP AT SEA
DR SINGH'S INSIGHTS
DR BINAY SINGH
SHIPS & RELATIONSHIPS
DR BINAY SINGH
MY FANTASTIC VOYAGE TO ODESSA
DR BINAY SINGH
THE ART OF GIVING
DR SINGH'S INSIGHTS
GIVE
DR BINAY SINGH
A MESSAGE TO YOUNG SEAFARERS
DR SINGH'S INSIGHTS
DR BINAY SINGH
Svetlana
my love forever
DR BINAY SINGH
THE ART OF MOTIVATIONAL SPEAKING
DR SINGH'S INSIGHTS
DR BINAY SINGH
BE REALISTIC IN YOUR Expectations
DR BINAY SINGH
The TRUE MEANING OF HOPE
DR BINAY SINGH
AVOIDING DISTRACTIONS ACHIEVING SUCCESS
DR SINGH'S INSIGHTS
DR BINAY SINGH
THE ART OF TIME MANAGEMENT
DR SINGH'S INSIGHTS
DR BINAY SINGH
THE ART OF DISCIPLINE
DR SINGH'S INSIGHTS
DR BINAY SINGH
Care WITH YOUR WORDS
DR BINAY SINGH
MR POSITIVE
DR SINGH'S GUIDE TO LIVING YOUR BEST LIFE
THE Magic OF MUSIC
DR SINGH'S INSIGHTS
DR BINAY SINGH
DR SINGH'S GUIDE TO REAL HAPPINESS
DR BINAY SINGH
THE NEW MARITIME WAY
DR BINAY SINGH
DR SINGH'S GUIDE TO REAL SUCCESS
DR BINAY SINGH
THE NEW ERA OF BUSINESS TRAINING
DR BINAY SINGH